The Masonic Genius of Robert Burns

Also from Westphalia Press
westphaliapress.org

The Masonic Genius of Robert Burns

An Address Delivered in Lodge "Quatuor Coronati," 2076, 4th March, 1892

by Bro. Benjamin Ward Richardson

WESTPHALIA PRESS

An Imprint of Policy Studies Organization

The Masonic Genius of Robert Burns: An Address Delivered in Lodge
"Quatuor Coronati," 2076, 4th March, 1892.

Westphalia Press
An imprint of Policy Studies Organization
1527 New Hampshire Ave. NW
Washington, D.C. 20036
info@ipsonet.org

ISBN-13: 978-1-63391-672-2
ISBN-10: 1-63391-672-3

Cover design by Jeffrey Barnes:
jbarnesbook.design

Daniel Gutierrez-Sandoval, Executive Director
PSO and Westphalia Press

Updated material and comments on this edition
can be found at the Westphalia Press website:
www.westphaliapress.org

ROBERT BURNS.

25th January, 1759 — 21st July, 1796.

THE MASONIC GENIUS OF

ROBERT BURNS,

BY BRO. BENJAMIN WARD RICHARDSON,

M.D., LL.D., F.R.S., F.S.A., &c.

AN ADDRESS

Delivered in Lodge "Quatuor Coronati," 2076,

4th March, 1892.

Reprinted from *Ars Quatuor Coronatorum*, with additional notes
by Bro. W. FRED VERNON, Kelso;

A picture of "Death and the Poet," by Bro. W. SIMPSON, R.I.,
and other illustrations.

KEBLE, TYPO., MARGATE.

THE MASONIC GENIUS OF
ROBERT BURNS.

THE MASONIC GENIUS OF
ROBERT BURNS.

BY BRO. BENJAMIN WARD RICHARDSON,

M.D., LL.D., F.R.S., F.S.A.

WORSHIPFUL MASTER AND BRETHREN,

WHEN I speak of the Masonic genius of Robert Burns, I mean that his genius, which is universally admitted, partakes of the genius of Masonic order or type. In this discourse I shall consider him first from this point of view. Next, I shall speak of his poetic genius as appealing primarily to the Masonic brotherhood, and as fostered and fed by that fraternity. I shall then proceed to treat of his love for the brotherhood as manifested in the productions of his poetic genius. Finally, I shall for a few moments dwell on the tendency and tenure of his work as Masonic in quality in the higher and nobler, shall I not say the highest and noblest, forms of Masonic liberty and moral amplitude. This will divide my subject into four sections or parts, and will enable brethren who may join in the discussion to fix on particular points as they follow what I shall venture to lay before them.

In studying the first section of this division—the genius of Masonry in relation to the natural genius of

the man—we must know the man from the first, know
him from his own heart. In an order or fraternity like
Masonry there is a true, a deep, and subtle genius which
holds it together; and that the order may be held
together there must be, in a greater or lesser degree, the
same kind of genius in every individual member. All
fraternities of might and effect and endurance, whether
they be considered good or bad by outsiders, must be
constructed on this plan. Orders, in fact, are composed
of men born to aptitudes befitting the order. There are,
of course, exceptions to this general rule. There are in
every fraternity members who are perfectly indifferent;
there are members who are merely converts; and there
are, in all great combinations, a few who may even be
inimical. But on the whole the strongest societies have
for their centre an overwhelming unity, at the head of
which are they who are particularly bound to the
principles that are at stake, and who come into the
mastery of those principles by what is naturally a
common bond. In this position Robert Burns stands as
regards the Masonic bond and unity. Masonry, when he
found it, was akin to his native genius; it was to him
that touch of nature which makes all akin.

For the birth of this sympathy we have to turn to
the best picture we can get of the poet while his nature
was being moulded into the form it took as Mason and
poet. Fortunately for us, owing to the interposition of a
very remarkable man, who is now too much forgotten,
we have an account of this period of the poet's life from

the poet himself.   The scholar who obtained this treasure
was Dr. John Moore, the father of that illustrious Sir
John Moore, hero of Corunna, on whom Wolfe wrote the
immortal poem beginning,—

> " Not a drum was heard nor a funeral note,
>   As his corse to the ramparts we hurried,
>   Not a soldier discharged a farewell shot
>   O'er the grave where our hero we buried."

Dr. Moore, whose life I have recently written, and
of whom I present three portraits for your inspection,
was by profession a physician, residing first in Glasgow
and finally in London; but he added to his Esculapian
gifts those of the traveller, the man of the world, and the
industrious writer.   He was in France with the Duke of
Hamilton before the days of the great Revolution, and
with the same clearness of foresight as his friend
Smollett, predicted the great event that must follow
from what he beheld in progress.   Again, he was in
Paris in the early days of the great Revolution itself ;
heard the first shots fired at the Tuilleries ; attended the
meetings of the National Assembly ; and left the finest
description of Marat, whom he knew personally, that has
ever been written on that famous infamous person.   His
journal of the days of the Revolution has been more
cribbed from, without acknowledgment, than most works
of original men.   But he was more than the journalist of
striking events ; he was himself an artist in letters, and
his story " Zelucco " was the inspiration of the poem
" Childe Harold," which Byron left to the admiring

world. Still further, Dr. Moore was of biographic taste,
and was anxious, on all suitable occasions, to get from
their prime sources the histories of remarkable men.
Thus it was he got from Robert Burns himself that
account of his, Burns', early days with which, I doubt
not, most of you are familiar. Gilbert Burns, brother of
the poet, says that in this narrative the poet set off some
of his early companions "in too consequential a manner,"
which is perhaps too true, for poets are apt to be poets
all over, in prose as in verse ; anyway, there is rendered
in this composition the fact which chiefly concerns us,
that companionship of the brotherly type was the early
love of the after Mason. Burns rejoiced in all social
gatherings, and cared nothing whatever for his daily
work when he was encircled, in the evening of the day,
with his friends whom, in love or in war, in song or in
story, he impetuously led. He was mystic from the
first, and breathed poetry before he knew it himself.
Like Pope :—

"He lisped in numbers, for the numbers came."

He was living at Tarbolton with his family when these
faculties, belonging to his seventeenth year, developed
themselves. He possessed, he says, a curiosity, zeal, and
intrepid dexterity that recommended him as a proper
second, and he felt as much pleasure in being in the
secret of half the loves of Tarbolton as ever did statesman
in knowing the intrigues of half the courts of Europe.
He felt that to the sons and daughters of poverty, "the
ardent hope, the stolen interview, the tender farewell,

are the greatest and most delicious parts of their enjoyments." This was a glance at the loves of the simple : he found it to apply, later on, to other mysteries, and in all cases his heart beat sympathetically to the sentiment.

In his nineteenth year he made a change in his life which is curious, symbolically, and perhaps had relation to after Masonic work of the speculative rather than the working character. He spent his nineteenth summer on a smuggling coast, a good distance from home, at a noted school, to learn mensuration, surveying, and dialling. Here, although he took part in scenes which had better have been avoided, he went on " with a high hand " at his geometry, " till the sun entered Virgo, which was always a carnival in his bosom," and then in a few weeks he left his school to return home. But he had considerably improved, and from his studies had certainly learned the use of the tools of a Mason, the rule, the compass, the level, and the skerritt.

All this was congenial towards Masonry in its form of speculative mystery, and we need not, therefore, be surprised that it was not long before he joined our ancient order. There was, at the time of his residence at Tarbolton, a Masonic Lodge called St. David's. The harmony which ought to exist in all Lodges of the Craft does not seem to have been perfect in this one. There had been another Lodge in Tarbolton, known as the St. James', and some discordant elements might have come down from that Lodge to the St. David's, which, for a

time, superseded it. Be that as it may, St. David's had
the honour of receiving the young Scottish poet into its
bosom. Burns was initiated in St. David's Lodge,
Tarbolton, on July 4th, 1781, he being then in his
twenty-third year. He became from that moment one
of the most devoted of Masons. In every way Masonry
was congenial to his mind. There was in it a spirit of
poetry which was all the sweeter to him because it was
concealed, and there was in it the fact of something done
which the best in the world copied from without knowing
the source of the inspiration; something like that which
Shelley afterwards, unconsciously as applied to this
subject, expressed in the exquisite song to the skylark :—

> " Like a poet hidden
>   In the light of thought,
> Singing hymns unbidden
>   Till the world is wrought
> To sympathy with hopes
>   And fears it heeded not."

and which Burns himself, in another form and measure,
expressed in the lines :—

> " The social, friendly, honest man,
>   Whate'er he be,
>   'Tis he fulfils great Nature's plan,
>   And none but he.

Burns had no sooner been initiated into Masonry than he
threw himself into work connected with it with his whole
heart. He found, nevertheless, that even among Masons
there may be discord. The old feud in the St. David's
Lodge increased, and came, at last, to such a pitch, that

a sharp division took place. In the year 1782 a number of the members of the Lodge seceded, and re-formed the old and almost forgotten St. James' Lodge of Tarbolton. Burns was amongst the seceders, and the newly-formed Lodge was destined, largely by his warm adhesion to it, to become one of the most famous historical Lodges Scottish Masonry ever boasted of. In this Lodge the poet found poetry, and in it, above all other prizes in the world, he found friendship. This fact leads me, naturally, to the second division of my paper: the fostering care he experienced as a poet from Masonic communion and enthusiasm.

By the time Burns joined the Lodge at Tarbolton he was a poet. He was not a poet of any wide renown, but he had written poems which some of his immediate circle of friends admired. His life up to this period, had been one of great strain and poverty. Born in a little cottage near Alloway Kirk, on the Doon, in Ayrshire, he had moved with his parents, when about seven years of age, to a farm in the parish of Ayr, called Mount-Oliphant. The farm was a ruinous affair. Here he worked on the land as a farm-boy for twelve years, after which the family passed, with no better fortune, to another farm, called Lochlea, in the parish of Tarbolton. Robert worked like the rest on this farm, but he was not exclusively engaged on farm labour. He went, as already told, to a sea coast place, Kirk Oswald, where he learned mensuration and other parts of arithmetic, which ultimately fitted him for the duties of an excise officer, and on the whole he picked up, at Kirk Oswald parish school, much information that served him well, with some tricks which did not serve him so well. He returned to the farm at Lochlea in his twentieth year; resumed work with his brother Gilbert, fell in love with a servant-maid, who jilted him, and led rather a wild life altogether. He and his brother tried their hands at flax-farming at the neighbouring village of Irvine, but during a New Year's day carousal the flax shop took fire and the whole stock was burnt up. Worse still, he got into bad company and into some disrepute.

Affairs at Lochlea went wrong with the excellent father of the poet, and in February, 1784, that good man died. The loss of his father incited the poet to a better life, and he and his brother took a larger farm at a place called Mossgiel, in the parish of Mauchline, near Tarbolton. The farming project failed, and good resolutions failed with it.

Our Brother the poet Burness, for he assumed the shorter name of Burns later on, was not at the moment of his career at which we have arrived, in a very happy or a very hopeful condition. He was poverty stricken, he was reckless, he had sent into the world an illegitimate child, and he was looked upon askance by those friends about him, who considered good morals the first of acquirements. Yet, with it all, he was not the absolute rake or prodigal which many have depicted him. He had availed himself of what advantages had

come before him. He had been for a short time blessed
by the instruction of a tutor named Murdock, from whom
he had learned among other things French, in which
language he greatly delighted, and he had gathered
together various classical and romantic books which he
read with the avidity a nature such as his alone
experiences. He had seen a little of the world at Kirk
Oswald, and he had acquired some knowledge of the
exact sciences. But above all, he was a poet and a
Mason.

Opinions have differed since his death, as they
differed in his own time and amongst his own friends, on
the point whether he did ill or well in joining the Lodge
in Tarbolton. Masonry was rather popular in Scotland,
but many thought that Robert Burness had joined it, not
because of the goodness there was in it, but because of

" The wale o' cocks for fun and drunkin'."

and in this view there was much sense for sober going
people, since it cannot be denied that Scotia's drink was
freely floated in the Lodges, when refreshment followed
the serious business of labour. Moreover, Robert himself,
at his twenty-third year, was a sufficient cause for alarm
amongst his friends. He was, physically, not well. He
had frequent dull headaches, and he was laying the seeds
for those conditions of faintness and palpitation of the
heart, which as his brother Gilbert tells us, were the
bodily burthens of after years.

He was, moreover, at this time, exceedingly unbridled
in his tastes. He was the prime spirit of a bachelor's

club, which, although the expenses were limited to
threepence per bachelor each night, was an assembly
that did not particularly raise him in public estimation ;
and he was always in love, not with one object of
affection, but with any and many, according to fancy,
investing, by his fancy, as Brother Gilbert informs us,
each of his loves with such a stock of charms, all drawn
from the plentiful stores of his imagination, that there
was often a great dissimilitude between the fair
captivator as she appeared to others and as she seemed
when bedecked with the attributes he gave to her. Up
to this time he was not given to intoxication, and when,
with his brother and family he entered into partnership
for the farm of Mossgiel, he contributed his share of
expenses, and lived most frugally. He had written
songs and other poetical pieces, which pleased those who
surrounded him, and the poems had accumulated to a
goodly number, but they were buried in necessity, and it
is very doubtful if by his own efforts they would ever
have been brought to light.

Day by day his adversity grew more and more
pressing. At last a crisis. Amongst his many loves
there was one who held to him to the end most firmly,
namely, Jean Armour, and with her love went so far it
could no longer be concealed. In the strait the lovers
came to a determination. They entered into a legal
acknowledgment of " an irregular private marriage," and
it was proposed that Burns should at once proceed to
Jamaica as an assistant overseer on the estate of Dr.

Douglas. Strangely, the parents of Jean Armour
objected to the acceptance of the marriage, under the
impression that great as had been the folly of Jean she
might live to do better than tie herself for life to
a scapegrace. To Burns this slight was intolerable,
although in a kind of contrition he seemed to bend to it.
It settled his resolve, he would go to Jamaica, and by
honest work would make up for past misfortune.

It happened that much time was required before he
could make a start for his new sphere of labour, and,
meanwhile, as preparations were going on something else
occurred, on which, as on a pivot, the fate and fame of
Robert Burns turned. In the Lodge of St. James,
Tarbolton, there was an important member, a writer to
the signet, living, near by, at Mauchline, and the
landlord of the farm of Mossgiel. This was Gavin
Hamilton, a happy-go-lucky, warmed-hearted, merry
fellow, much attached to the ploughman poet, some of
whose effusions he had heard in song at least, and
towards whom he entertained a sincere admiration.
Hamilton suggested that Burns should collect and
publish an edition of his poems, and that the expense
should be met by a subscription. The plan was after the
poet's own desire, I may say fervent desire. He longed
to leave his name to posterity, and, in fact, cared for
little else. The ordinary life was to him already a
burden, but the idea of immortal fame was something
worth living for, and was even worth the weariness of

the world. He seized, therefore, on the proposal with avidity. It was early in the year of 1786, and his vessel for Jamaica would not sail until November; let then the proposal, of all things, be carried out.

With all his faults Burns stood high in his Lodge of St. James, at Tarbolton. In 1784 he was made Depute Master, Major General Montgomery being Worshipful Master. In 1785 he attended Lodge nine times, and acted many times, if not every time, as Master. In 1786 he attended nine times, and at the second meeting, held on March the first, passed and raised his brother Gilbert. How well he fulfilled the duties of his office is told by no less a person than the famous metaphysical scholar, Dugald Stewart, who had a neighbouring country residence at Catrine. Stewart specially commends the ready wit, happy conception and fluent speech of the Depute Master of St. James' Lodge. There can be no doubt that the Lodge, in return, became responsible altogether for the issue of the first volume of poems of Robert Burns, not as an official act, but as an act of personal friendship for their talented brother; and, under their initiative, he went to Kilmarnock, in order to see through the Press the new and now precious first edition of poems dated April 16th, 1786. Whilst residing in Kilmarnock, he met with the warmest reception and encouragement from the Masonic brethren there. He became a visitor of St. John's Lodge at once, and on the 26th of October, 1786, was admitted an honorary member. The brethren of this Lodge assisted him also

substantially in his venture.   Brother Major Parker
subscribed to thirty-five copies of the book, and Robert
Muir, another of the brethren of St. John's, to seventy-
five copies, whilst a third brother, John Wilson, printed
and published the volume.   In short, the first edition
was in every sense such a Masonic edition, we may
almost declare that but for Masonry the poems of Robert
Burns, now disseminated over all the world, had merely
been delivered to the winds as the mental meanderings of
a vulgar and disreputable Scotch boor.   Thus, the genius
of Masonry discovered and led forth the genius of one of
the greatest of the poets of Scotland.

The good genius of masonry did not end at this
point.   It brought out the volume of poems, and made
the author master of a little balance of money for his
work ; but, alas, the return was not sufficient to prevent
the evil fate that would separate him from all he loved
best.   He was still pursued by ill fortune.   His little bit
of luggage was on its way to Greenock, he following it,
playing at hide-and-seek, and wishing Jamaica at the
bottom of the sea, when a letter reached him again from a
brother mason, a gentle blind brother, with a taste for
the muses, Brother Dr. Blacklock, suggesting that a new
edition of the Kilmarnock poems should be published in
Edinburgh, and that their author should go to that fair
city and superintend the undertaking.   Burns at once
responded, and on the 26th of November, instead of being
on the sea for the West Indies, he was in the modern
Athens, and in the midst of enthusiastic friends, all

warmed to friendship by the mystical fire. Here things
went grandly. Henry Mackenzie, a good mason and
good writer, author of "The Man of Feeling," announced
through a paper, called the *Lounger*, that a new poet had
been born to Scotland; and David Ramsay, editor of the
Evening Courant, another brother, represented him to his
world of letters as :—

"The Prince of Poets, an o' pleughmen."

And so this Prince of Poets ploughed his way into the
best circles of Auld Reekie. He was at once great in
the Masonic Lodges. The Worshipful Grand Master
Charteris, at the Lodge of St. Andrew, proposed as a
toast, "Caledonia and Caledonia's Bard Brother Burns,"
"a toast," the Bard writes, "which rang through the
whole assembly, with multiplied honours and repeated
acclamations; while he, having no idea such a thing
would happen, was "downright thunderstruck, and
trembling in every nerve" made the best return in his
power. Jamaica vanished!

Early next year, February 1st, 1787, the Edinburgh
edition of the poems, being well in hand, Burns was
admitted by unanimous consent, a brother of the
Canongate Kilwinning Lodge, in which on the first of
the following month the Master—Fergusson of Craigdarrock—dignified him as Poet Laureate of the brotherhood, and assigned him a special poet's throne. The
time now quickly arrived, April 21st, for the appearance
of the new volume. The members of the Caledonian
Hunt, under the leadership of Lord Glencairn, to whom

the poet was introduced by Brother Dalrymple, subscribed liberally, and altogether a subscription list of 2,000 copies was secured, the Masonic influence again leading the way. "Surely," says an anonymous writer on this subject, "a son of the Rock," as he styled himself, but whom I have since found to have been Mr. James Gibson, of Liverpool, and not himself a Mason, "surely never book came out of a more Masonic laboratory. Publisher, printer, portrait painter, and engraver of the portrait were a rare class of men—all characters in their way—and all Masons." Creech was the publisher, Smellie was the printer, Alexander Nasmyth was the painter, and Bengo was the engraver, each and all Masons of the staunchest quality. Under such support the poems were bound to go, and they went, carrying their author with them into the glory he most desired.

As it is not my business to dwell on the life of Burns out of its Masonic encircling, I need not to dwell on his later career; his flirtations with Clarinda, his love with Mary Campbell; his journeyings and jollifications; his melancholy and his remorse; his marriage with Jane Armour; his failure as a farmer at Ellisland; his entrance into the excise; his residence at Dumfries; his final intemperance and his early death on July 21st, 1796. Let it be sufficient to add that St. Abbs' Lodge at Eyemouth made him a Royal Arch Mason, omitting his fees and considering themselves honoured by having a man of such shining abilities as one of their companions; that when he settled in Dumfries, the Lodge of St. Andrew received him with open arms ; and that to him ever, to use the words of Mr. Gibson, "Masonry held out an irresistible hand of friendship."

I come now to the third point to which, Worshipful Master, I would direct the mind of the Lodge—the love of the poet for the brotherhood, as represented in his poetical works.

There are at least eight poems in which Masonry is directly connected with the theme of the poem or song. A short epistle in verse to Brother Dr. Mackenzie,[1] informing him that St. James' Lodge will meet on St. John's day, is racy and refers to a controversy on morals which had been going on in the little circle. An elegy to Tam Samson relates to a famous seedsman, sportsman, and curler, but above all a Mason of the Kilmarnock Lodge, and a sterling friend of all who knew him in friendship's mysteries.

> " The brethren o' the mystic level
> May hing their heads in waefu' bevel,
> While by their nose the tears will revel
> Like ony bead.
> Death's gien the Lodge an unco' devel,
> Tam Samson's dead."

In like manner, but with a tender sweetness and more subdued verse, he writes another elegy on one to whom he was bound by the mystic tie, Sir James Hunter Blair. The poem is finely conceived. The poet supposes himself wandering in some secluded haunt :—

[1] See *Ars Quatuor Coronatorum*, iii., 103,

> " The lamp of day, with ill-presaging glare,
>> Dim, cloudy, sinks beneath the western wave,
> Th' inconsistant blast howls through the darkening air,
>> And hollow, whistles in the rocky cave."

The moon then rises " in the livid east," and among the cliffs the stately form of Caledonia appears " drooped in pensive woe." " The lightning of her eyes " is imbued in tears; her spear is reversed; her banner at her feet. So attuned she sings her sorrow for the loss of her son and the grief of her sons, not omitting the sons of light and science :

> " A weeping country joins a widow's tear,
>> The helpless poor mix with the orphan's cry ;
> The drooping arts surround their patron's bier,
>> And grateful science heaves the heartfelt sigh."

In an epistle to his publisher, William Creech, whose Masonic virtues I have already noted, we get just a glimpse into Kilwinning Lodge, Edinburgh, when Willie, that is Creech, is on his travels in London. " Willie's awa'."

> " Now worthy Gregory's latin face,
>> Tytler's and Greenfield's modest grace,
>> Mackenzie, Stewart, sic a brace,
>> They a' maun meet some ither place.
>>> Willie's awa' !"

Gregory of the Latin face was the famous Dr. James Gregory, perhaps the purest Latin writer medicine ever produced in his country, but better known as the inventor of the most nauseous, and yet one of the most useful medicines—Gregory's powder. Greenfield was the eminent Professor of Rhetoric; and Stewart the illustrious Dugald.

"Willie brew'd a peck of maut" is a Masonic song of genius. Willie was Brother William Nicol, of the High School, Edinburgh, with whom the poet made a tour to the Highlands; Allan was Brother Allan Masterton, and Rob was Brother the Poet himself; three Masons holding an informal Lodge at Nicol's place at Moffat during the summer vacation. It was such a joyous meeting that each in his own way celebrated it; Willie—Nicol—with the maut, Rob—Burns—with the song, and Allan—Masterton—with the music.

The poem of Death and Dr. Hornbook is of Masonic origin. Hornbook was Brother Wilson, schoolmaster of Tarbolton, and a member of the Lodge, who took to reading medical books and dabbling in physic. One night, aiter going from labour to refreshment, Wilson paraded his medical knowledge and skill too loudly to miss the watchful Robert, and Robert, on his way home, was accompanied by this mixture of pedantry and physic to a certain point, where they shook hands and parted. Left alone, the old fancies of goblins and spirits came on the poet; Death came, and after a conversation with that reaper, the flowing satire on the poor dominie was composed. These circumstances, Gilbert Burns says, his brother related as he repeated the verses to him the next afternoon, while Gilbert was holding the plough and Robert was letting the water off the field beside him. How the poem took when it was first published is matter of history. It settled poor Brother Wilson for good as a self-constituted doctor at Tarbolton, the verse beginning with the words, " A bonnie lass ye kenn'd her name," telling with potent effect.

Wilson, I believe, was the only Mason Burns lampooned, and he without enmity. Wilson, however, had to leave Tarbolton, and, retreating to Glasgow, became clerk of the Gorbals parish, and lived until 1839, half-a-century after the Tarbolton exodus. Cromek, one of the writers on Burns,[1] who knew Wilson in his later days, says Wilson had so little pedantry about him that a man who never read the poem would scarcely discover any, and I have heard others who also knew him make the same observation.

The song entitled " The sons of old Killie," beginning—

> " Ye sons of old Killie assembled by Willie
>   To follow the noble vocation,
>   Your thrifty old mother has scarce such another
>   To sit in that honouréd station.
>   I've little to say, but only to pray,
>   As praying 's the *ton* of your fashion ;
>   A prayer from the muse you well may excuse,
>   'Tis seldom her favourite passion."

[1] Cromek, a Yorkshireman, an art publisher, engraver, and in some sense, an artist, went to Scotland, ten years after the poet's death, to collect materials for a volume on Burns, as a kind of supplement to four volumes that had already been written by Dr. Currie. The volume was entitled the " Reliques of Burns," and was published by Cadell and Davies in 1808.

was produced at a festival of the Kilmarnock Lodge, Willie aforesaid being Bro. William Parker, the Worshipful Master.

I must not weary you with too many of these snatches of Masonic light from our immortal brother, but it would be impossible to omit the one jewel of jewels of song which he sang, or rather chanted than sang, to the tune of " Good night, and joy be wi' you a'," at the meeting of St. James' Lodge, Tarbolton, at the moment when his little box of luggage was on its way to Greenock, and he, very soon as he believed, was bound to follow it. We can picture to ourselves the Lodge, Major-General James Montgomery, W.M., in the chair; the Wardens in place; the brethren round the board, and the Depute Master, heart-broken, thinking it the last song he shall ever compose in dear old Scotland. We may picture the meeting, but the emotion of that moment can be but a faint expression.

> " Adieu ! a heart-warm fond adieu !
>   Dear brothers of the mystic tie !
> Ye favour'd, ye enlighten'd few,
>   Companions of my social joy.
> Though I to foreign lands must hie,
>   Pursuing fortune's slidd'ry ba'.
> With melting heart, and brimful eye,
>   I'll mind you still, though far awa'.
>
> Oft have I met your social band,
>   And spent the cheerful festive night
> Oft, honoured with supreme command,
>   Presided o'er the sons of light,

And by that heiroglyphic bright,
  Which none but craftsmen ever saw !
Strong memory on my heart shall write,
  Those happy scenes when far awa' !

May freedom, harmony, and love,
  Unite you in the grand design,
Beneath the omniscient eye above,
  The glorious Architect divine !
That you may keep the unerring line,
  Still rising by the plummet's law,
Till order bright completely shine
  Shall be my prayer when far awa'.

And you farewell ! whose merits claim
  Justly that highest badge to wear,
Heaven bless your honoured noble name
  To Masonry and Scotia dear.
A last request permit me here,
  When yearly ye assemble a',
One round—I ask it with a tear—
  To him, the Bard, that's far awa'."

The tear was quenched ; in pursuing "fortune's slidd'ry ba'" the poet was led to Edina instead of Jamaica ; yet even this not without one sorrow, one tear ; for on the very day he entered the beautiful city to be for a flicker her hero of ploughmen, William Wallace, Grand Master of Scotland, "To Masonry and Scotia dear," ascended to the Grand Lodge above.

I pass to the last fragment of my discourse, namely, the tendency and tenure of the genius of Robert Burns as a Masonic poet. With the deepest admiration for a poet whose words have been familiar to me and whose sentiments have touched my heart from the earliest days of my recollection, I am not blind to his sins of emotion. I know his faults. But in all the poet said, and, I believe, thought, about the principles of Masonry, he kept by the unerring line, as if indeed the eye omniscient were upon him; and as if in pure Masonry, in its tenets, its symbolisms, and, in the best sense, its practices, there is a secret spell on the mind and heart, in which the mind and heart must live and move and have its being.

The best idea of Masonry on these foundations found its noblest utterance, from our poet brother, in his peroration to St. John's Lodge, Kilmarnock.

> " Ye powers who preside o'er the wind and the tide,
>   Who marked out each element's border;
> Who founded this frame with beneficent aim,
>   Whose sovereign statute is order.
> Within this dear mansion may wayward contention
>   Or withering envy ne'er enter;
> May secrecy round be the mystical bound,
>   And brotherly love be the centre."

Worshipful Sir, let that peroration be mine to-night, to Quatuor Coronati!

The WORSHIPFUL MASTER having called for comments on the interesting paper which had just been read,

BRO. GOULD felt that there could be little to say, except to express his pleasure, and he was sure he might add the pleasure of all the brethren present, at the treat which Bro. Richardson had afforded them. He would, however, in passing, make one remark as to the supposed and so often alleged laureateship of the Canongate Kilwinning Lodge. There was nothing to show that such a title had ever been conferred upon the poet until after his death, and it certainly was in no way borne out by the minutes of the Lodge. He begged to move a vote of thanks to Brother Richardson.

This was seconded by BRO. WESTCOTT, and supported by BRO. CHAMBERLIN, himself a member of the Canongate Kilwinning, and after a few remarks from the Chair, carried by acclamation.

ADDENDUM.

BY BRO. W. FRED VERNON.

Having been requested to make a few remarks on the eloquent prelection which our talented Brother Dr. Richardson has delivered on "the Masonic Genius of Robert Burns," I feel I cannot allow the opportunity to pass without expressing, in the first place, my warm thanks to him for his very interesting sketch of the Masonic career of Scotia's Bard, and in the second place without subjecting some of his remarks to a measure of criticism. But before doing so I would add my commendations to those of the other brethren, and must congratulate the learned doctor upon the admirable apothegm he has given us in his exordium, viz., " Orders are composed of men born to aptitudes befitting the order," which is, I think, a very happy and true rendering of the axiom previously formulated, that " In an order or fraternity like Masonry there is a true, a deep, and subtle genius which holds it together : and that the Order may be held together there must be, in a greater or lesser degree, the same kind of genius in every individual member," from which he deduces the truth that "Masonry was alike to Burns' native genius, it was to him that touch of nature which makes all akin." It was this "one touch of nature," this inborn feeling or perception of the universality of the brotherhood of man so frequently expressed in his works, which constituted his Masonic genius. For instance, we have in the following lines, which are most characteristic of the writer, the fundamental principle or spirit of Masonry :—

> " A' ye whom social pleasure charms,
> Whose heart the tide of kindness warms,
> Wha hold your being on the terms,
> > ' *Each aid the others,*'
> Come to my bowl, come to my arms,
> > My friends, my BROTHERS."

And again in the manly lines of the song beginning " Is there for honest poverty, wha hangs his head and a' that," this feeling finds expression in the noble aspiration :—

> " Then let us pray that come it may—
> As come it will for a' that—
> That sense and worth o'er a' the earth
> May bear the gree, and a' that,

> For a' that, and a' that,
>   It's comin' yet for a' that,
> That man to man, the warld o'er,
>   Shall brithers be and a' that."

Herein lies the great secret of Burns' universal popularity : not only his love of nature, which is a common attribute of all poets, but by reason of his intense love of human nature, he was the more richly endowed with a deeper sympathy with humanity, which enabled him to strike a chord in all our hearts which vibrates in unison with that which thrilled his own, deepening our sympathies towards our fellow men and enlarging our hearts in universal love. This is, without a doubt, the keystone of the great arch of Burns' Masonic genius.

Our poet's family name, as Brother Richardson observes, was not always Burns but was originally Burness, and it may interest the brethren to know that on the 25th of May, 1786, he announced to the members of the Lodge at Tarbolton that he intended assuming in future the shorter name of Burns, and he accordingly signed the minutes that evening for the first time by the now familiar and world-famous name of Robert Burns. Brother Richardson informs us of his regular attendance in the Lodge, and mentions that he attended to his duties nine times in the year 1785 and the same number of times in 1786, and we find the minute book bearing ample and valuable testimony to his assiduity as a Mason, for page after page is filled with his hand writing and his autograph as Depute Master, thus making the little volume of this out-of-the-way Lodge more valuable than the records of the most ancient Lodge in the world.

We come now to Burns' appearance in Edinburgh amongst the brethren there, and here I would take objection to the statement that on the 1st of March, 1787, Bro. Alexander Fergusson of Craigdarrock, the Master of Canongate Kilwinning Lodge, "dignified him as Poet Laureate of the Brotherhood, and assigne l him a special poet's throne." There is nothing to warrant this assertion, which has been frequently made and as frequently contradicted, but the idea is a popular one and forms the subject of a well-known picture by the late Bro. Stewart Watson which has done much to perpetuate the fallacy.[1]   As Bro. Richardson says, Burns was assumed a member of Canongate Kilwinning Lodge on the 1st of February, 1787, the minutes of the meeting being in the following terms : " The Right Worshipful Master, having observed that Brother Burns was at present in the Lodge, who is well known as a great Poetic Writer, and for a late publication of his Works, which have been universally

[1] Since writing the above I have received a little book from Bro. William Officer, P.M. The Lodge of Edinburgh (Mary's Chapel), No. 1, etc., etc., entitled " Burns, Poet Laureate of Canongate Kilwinning—a myth," being a series of letters between himself and Bro. Allan Mackenzie, the historian of Lodge Canongate Kilwinning, in which he indubitably proves the position taken up by Bro. Mackenzie and others who maintain that Burns was installed laureate of the Lodge to be untenable.

commended, and submitted that he should be assumed a Member of this Lodge, which was unanimously agreed to, and he was assumed accordingly," but the minutes contain no reference to his having been laureated by the Lodge. Bro. Murray Lyon, in his well-known History, says, " The 1st of March, 1787, is mentioned by Masonic writers as the date of the scene which has been pourtrayed by the artist. But neither the minutes of that date, nor of any other during Burns' lifetime contain any record whatever of the existence of such an office as Laureate of the Lodge or of that distinction being conferred on Burns. The first mention in Canongate Kilwinning minutes of this office having been held by the Poet is found under date February 9th, 1815, when the Lodge resolved to open a subscription among its members to aid in the erection of a ' Mausoleum to the memory of Robert Burns, who was a member and Poet Laureate of this Lodge,' " a very evident afterthought which is repeated in the minute of the 9th of June, 1815, and again in that of the 16th of January, 1835, which chronicles the appointment of Brother James Hogg, the " Ettrick shepherd," to the " honorary office of Poet Laureate of the Lodge, which had been ' in abeyance since the death of the immortal Brother Robert Burns.' "[1]

Dr. Richardson, like a skilful physician, delicately touches a tender spot, when he says he knows our poet's faults and is " not blind to his sins of emotion." Some persons there are who have not this delicacy, and I am

See Lyon's *History*, page 333.

sorry to say there are many who do not deal so gently or kindly with our brother's memory as he would have done himself in the case of an erring brother, for does he not counsel us to do so in these well-known lines ?—

> " Then gently scan your brother man,
>   Still gentler sister woman ;
> Though they' may gang a kennin' wrang
>   To step aside is human ;
> One point must still be greatly dark,
>   The moving *Why* they do it,
> And just as lamely can ye mark
>   How far, perhaps, they rue it.
>
> Who made the heart, 'tis He alone,
>   Decidedly can try us,
> He knows each chord—its various tone,
>   Each spring—its various bias ;
> Then at the balance let's be mute,
>   We never can adjust it ;
> What's done we partly may compute,
>   But know not what's resisted."

Let us exercise towards his memory then that charity which he inculcates in the above and which we, as Masons, profess to admire and cultivate, and leave, as he himself would have us leave, the judgment of every action to the Maker of the heart. Like Dr. Richardson I, too, from my earliest years have been acquainted with the works of the poet, and have diligently and lovingly studied them, and in my maturer years have sighed over the short sad story of his life, but the more I study his rich legacy of song the more

I appreciate " the God-made king," and thank the Giver
of all good who

> " —— sent his singers upon earth,
> With songs of sadness and of mirth,
> That they might teach the hearts of men,
> And bring them back to heaven again."

and not the least among them " To charm, to strengthen,
and to teach," is our poet brother, Robert Burns.

One more point and I have done, and sorry am I to
have occasion to note this point ; it is in reference to a
certain obnoxious volume of doggerel which is palmed
upon an inconsiderate world as Burns' " Merry Muses."
I would humbly suggest that the mere fact that some of
the contents of the book are in the handwriting of Allan
Cunningham is no conclusive proof that Burns ever
wrote a single line of it, because Allan Cunningham was
not acquainted with Burns, he was not the poet's friend ;
he was a boy of a little over ten years of age when the
poet died, and it is not likely that Burns would contract
a friendship with a youth of that age, or confide to him
songs of such a nature that the rare volume must needs
be concealed as a forbidden book to the eyes of childhood.
No! a thousand times no! I have seen and read the
filthy volume, and there is not one redeeming point in it.
One can tolerate smut when it is classical or witty, as in
the *Decameron* and some of our ancient masters, but when
it is unaccompanied by wit or cleverness or sense or
reason it is intolerable : and the halting lines, the
spurious rhymes, and contemptible stuff contained in this

volume stamp it as the offspring, not of a genius like Burns, but of some grovelling prurient incestuous mind or minds. Like Thomas, I doubt and will not believe until I have ample proof, and not till I see the lines in his own holograph, or with his name adhibited in his well-known hand will I be convinced that our much loved poet, and much maligned by the "unco' guid," ever penned these foul effusions. The songs of our country were dross and worse until the advent of Burns; it was he who, by the refining power of his divine genius, turned them into pure gold, and gave them a free unsullied gift to his country-men, and I cannot entertain in my own mind for a single moment that he, who had done so much towards purifying the literature of his country, would ever leave it such a degrading legacy as the "Merry Muses," which I maintain is frequently falsely and calumniously, but I trust more often thoughtlessly, ascribed to him. We know but too well that there are wine stains and other splashes on his regal robes, but even in his cups he never degraded his high office, he never deliberately doffed and dragged those robes through the mire. What says his centenary poet?

> "Though he may yield
> Hard-pressed, and wounded fall
> Forsaken on the field;
> His regal vestments soiled;
> His crown of half its jewels spoiled;
> He is a king for all."[1]

[1] "Ode on the Centenary of Burns," Crystal Palace Prize Poem, 25th January, 1859, by Isa. Craig.

I am sorry that 1 am compelled to speak so strongly, but I feel strongly, and think that as this paper has been devoted to the " Masonic Genius of Burns," it is a fit and proper place to enter once for all a protest against the calumny which so often ascribes this foul doggerel to the Bard of Scotland. In conclusion, I feel that we all owe Bro. Dr. Richardson a deep debt of gratitude for his admirable and eloquent address on " The Masonic Genius of Robert Burns."

BURNS' MOTHER LODGE.

Robert Burns was in the twenty-third year of his age and living with his father at the farm of Lochlea, in the parish of Tarbolton, when on the 4th July, 1781, he was entered an apprentice in the Lodge St. David, Tarbolton. The history of this Lodge is briefly as follows :—Lodge Kilwinning, fondly called " Mother Kilwinning " by its subordinate Lodges, claiming to be the oldest Lodge in Scotland, still held aloof from Grand Lodge, and arrogated to itself the right of granting charters of constitution and holding a jurisdiction over other Lodges, and a Lodge was formed in 1781 in the village of Tarbolton by authority of a charter from Kilwinning, and was named St. James.

Some difference of opinion amongst the brethren in 1773 caused a disruption, and the seceding portion formed themselves into a new Lodge and called it St. David. These two Lodges continued in opposition till 1781, when they amalgamated, the united Lodges taking St. David as their patronymic. It was a few weeks after this new arrangement that Burns was initiated ; the Brother who had the honour of thus ushering into the light of Masonry our illustrious Brother, was one Alexander Wood, a tailor, of Tarbolton, and on the 1st of October of the same year Burns was passed and raised. The element of dissention seemingly had not died out, for the union of the two Lodges did not last long, and a split again took place in 1782, when Burns and the other seceders reformed St. James, which still exists, its present number on the roll of Grand Lodge being 135, its former number having been 178. St. David's did not seem to prosper, and was finally erased from the roll in 1843. In July, 1784, Burns was elected Deputy Master, and held this office for several years, as evidenced by his signature being frequently appended to the minutes. He was present, and in all probability officiated, at the initiation, passing and raising of his brother Gilbert, on the 14th of March, 1786.

BURNS' EXALTATION TO THE R.A.

In the course of his Border Tour in 1787, Burns and his friend Robert Ainslie, a young lawyer of Edinburgh and a member of St. Luke's Lodge there, arrived at Eyemouth on the 18th May and put up at the house of Brother William Grieve, whom Burns describes as "a joyous, warmhearted, jolly, clever fellow—takes a hearty glass, and sings a good song." In connection with the Lodge of St. Abbe of Eyemouth there was a Royal Arch

Chapter, or Encampment as it is called, and Mr. Grieve was one of its most active members, and no doubt through his influence a meeting was specially convened and Burns and Ainslie were made Royal Arch Masons, the brotherly record of the occasion which reflects so much credit on the brethren of the Encampment being as follows :—

"Eyemouth, 19th May, 1787.

" At a General Encampment held this day, the following brethren were made Royal Arch Masons, namely : Robert Burns, from the Lodge St. James, Tarbolton, Ayrshire; and Robert Ainslie from the Lodge of St. Luke, Edinburgh, by James Carmichael, William Grieve, Daniel Dow, John Clay, Robert Grieve, &c., &c.

Robert Ainslie paid one guinea admission dues; but on account of Robert Burns' remarkable poetical genius, the Encampment unanimously agreed to admit him gratis, and considered themselves honoured by having a man of such shining abilities for one of their companions."

THE INAUGURATION OF BURNS AS POET
LAUREATE OF THE CANONGATE KILWINNING LODGE.

This well-known painting, by Mr. Stewart Watson, which finds a fitting home on the walls of the Board Room of the Grand Lodge of Scotland, is familiar to most Scotsmen by the many reproductions they may have seen in lodge rooms or in the homes of Scottish masons.

But while it is of considerable merit as a work of art, it is
as an historic memento of an incident in the life of Burns
of no value whatever, seeing that the ceremony never took
place,[1] nevertheless it is of great interest and value inas-
much it gives in one comprehensive group the poet surrounded by his contemporaries. Here we see, at a glance,
the sort of men who were for a time his friends and
companions, the representative men of the intellectual
world with whom he came in contact during his sojourn
in Edinburgh during his visit in 1786-87.

The scene is represented as taking place in the
lodge room of Canongate Kilwinning, St. John Street,
Edinburgh, Burns is standing on the steps of the däis
from which the R.W. Master, Alexander Ferguson, Esq.,
of Craigdarrock, is represented as holding out the
laureate's wreath to him, and the distinguished visiting
brethren on the Master's left are Lords Elcho, Tor-
phichen, Glencairn, Eglinton and Buchan ; those on the
right hand being Sir William Forbes, Sir John White-
ford, Mr. Dalrymple, of Orangefield, Mr. Millar, of
Dalsminton, and Mr. Charles More, of the Royal Bank,
Deputy Master of the Lodge. Immediately below seated
at the secretary's table we have in front Lord Monboddo
and leaning on the back of the chair William Mason,
Grand Secretary ; opposite Lord Monboddo is the Hon.
Henry Erskine, the brother of whom we have the back
view being the secretary, John Mercer. Midway between
the two tables in the foreground the officer of the lodge,

[1] See footnote *ante* p. 30.

Kenneth Love, is seen taking some clothing from a box,
and behind him with arm resting on the table intently
observing the ceremony is Lord Napier; and leaning
back upon the same table is the portly form of Captain
Francis Grose, the antiquary, to whom Dr. James Gregory
is speaking. Behind Dr. Gregory is Mr. Alexander
Wood, Surgeon; in front of whom stands, hat in hand,
Sir James Hunter Blair; beside whom, with hands
clasped upon his apron, is James Boswell, of Auchinlock,
and beyond him stands Alexander Nasymth, the artist.
Seated a little in front of him is Professor Dugald
Stewart, while leaning upon the table is William Smellie,
and next to him may be seen Peter Williamson talking to
William Creech, the publisher, who is seated at the end of
the table. The prominent figure in the centre with
bâton of office holding the ribbon and jewel in his left hand
is William Dunbar, writer to the Signet, the S.W.
of the lodge; behind whom stands William Nichol, of
the High School, and behind these two may be seen the
head of another classical teacher, William Cruikshank.
Between the Senior Warden and Burns, in front of the
treasurer's table, with head resting on hand, is Henry
Mackenzie, author of "The Man of Feeling," facing the
treasurer, George Spankie, next to whom is seated Baron
Norton, to whom Lord Kenmure is speaking, while
behind conversing with Lord Buchan may be seen Burns'
intimate friend Alexander Cunningham. Talking to one
of the musicians is Allan Masterton, the Allan who "cam
tae pree" Willie Nichol's browst, it was he who composed

the music to this song[1], and the violinist is Signor Stabilini; the other members of the orchestra being James Tytler, who performed on the Irish bagpipe, Thomas Neill, John Dhu, Alexander Campbell, organist, John Campbell, Samuel Clark, George Cranstown, J. G. C. Schetky with the violincello, all well-known musicians, of Edinburgh. In the background, beneath the portrait of St. Clair of Roslyn, stands John Millar, advocate, the Junior Warden of the lodge, while below him looking up is Captain Bartlet, of Milton House; behind him is Robert Ainslie, Writer to the Signet, and in front "dispensing the elements" from a capacious punch bowl is William Woods, a leading actor of the Edinburgh Theatre. To describe all these characters in detail would take a volume, and to a little volume entitled, "A Winter with Burns," published in 1846 by Bro. James Marshall, S.S.C., which contains a key to the portraits, we are indebted for the information given above.

[1] See *ante* p. 22.

BURNS' COTTAGE.
The "Auld Clay Biggin" as it used to be.

Ode — Bruce's address to
his troops at
Bannockburn — Tune Scots Gordon

Scots, wha hae wi' Wallace bled;
Scots, wham Bruce has aften led;
Welcome to your gory bed,
Or to glorious victorie.

Robt Burns

The verse is from the original in the possession of the late Robert Wallace of Kelly, Esq. The signature is from a letter to Captain Miller of Dalswinton, accompanying the Ode.

AUTOCRAPH OF
BURNS
in the Bible presented to
"HICHLAND MARY."

Vol. 1., b.1.

Vol. 2., p. 1.

" p.2.

" p. 2.

This Bible is in two small volumes: they were brought from Canada in 1840 by the late Robert Weir, Stationer, of Queen Street, Glasgow, and deposited in the Burns' Monument at Ayr. The half obliterated Masonic Mark renders them doubly interesting to Masons.

44

DEATH AND THE POET.
By Bro. W. Simpson, R.I.

JEWEL
said to have belonged to Robert Burns,
exhibited in Lodge " Quatuor Coronati "
1st March, 1889.

Featured Titles from
Westphalia Press

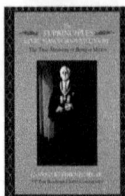

The 33 Principles Every Mason Should Live By: The True Meaning of Being a Mason by C. Fred Kleinknecht Jr.

These 33 principles are what all Freemasons should live by, they are the true meaning of Freemasonry. This book will not only benefit the Freemason but everyone can profit. I pass this along to you as a record of the Kleinknecht legacy of leadership.

Freemasonry, Politics and Rijeka (Fiume) (1785-1944) by Ljubinka Toseva Karpowicz

The greater part of the work concentrates on the efforts of Italian Irredentism in Rijeka in which intellectuals and Masons from Rijeka and Italy played a leading role. Some chapters analyze the work of Italian Masonry during the Fascist era, the military coup against the Free State of Fiume and much more.

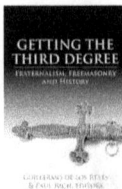

Getting the Third Degree: Fraternalism, Freemasonry and History Edited by Guillermo De Los Reyes and Paul Rich

As this engaging collection demonstrates, the doors being opened on the subject range from art history to political science to anthropology, as well as gender studies, sociology and more. The organizations discussed may insist on secrecy, but the research into them belies that.

Dudley Wright: Writer, Truthseeker & Freemason by John Belton

Dudley Wright (1868-1950) was an Englishman who took a universalist approach to the various great Truths of Life, he travelled though many religions in his life and wrote about them all, but was probably most at home with Islam. As a professional journalist he made his living where he could.

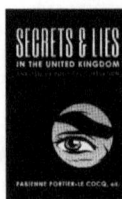

Secrets & Lies in the United Kingdom: Analysis of Political Corruption
Edited by by Fabienne Portier-Le Cocq

Secrets & Lies in the United Kingdom: Analysis of Political Corruption lifts the shroud of secrecy in the United Kingdom in relation to modern freemasonry in Scotland in the late-18th century, the 'Stolen Generations' in Australia from the early 1900s to the late 1970s, and so much more.

An Introduction to the Formation of Freemasonry in the United States of America: The Constellation of the Brotherhood by Larissa P. Watkins

The Constellation of the Brotherhood is another stellar reference resource by bibliographer Larissa Watkins. It encompasses the developmental history of the Grand Masonic Bodies in the United States for each state. It will be a boon to researchers, Masonic libraries as well as public and university libraries and others.

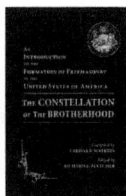

History of Freemasonry in the State of New York by Ossian Lang

Social history as a corrective to a historiography is often too limited to diplomacy and wars. It began an upward trajectory as early as the 1930s, but it remains constrained by the frustrating cost and availability of materials that even great research libraries lack. This volume is a case in point.

Between Conflict and Conformity:: Freemasonry During the Weimar Republic and the "Third Reich" by Ralf Melzer, Translated by Glenys A. Waldman

Freemasonry during the Weimar Republic and the 'Third Reich'... One might ask, "Is that a chapter of forgotten persecution or a legend of persecution?" After extensive research in archives in Berlin, Moscow, and Washington, D.C., the author has determined that the answer would have to be: "Neither, nor; yet some of both."

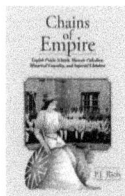

Chains of Empire: English Public Schools, Masonic Children, Historical Causality, and Imperial Clubdom

The British Empire's and the English public schools' peculiar system of rituals and rewards had more in common than has been realized. In Chains of Empire, Paul Rich related this to controversies about historical causality, morphic resonance, chaos, and the claims to influence of other bastions of the Imperial ethos.

Freemasonry: A French View by Roger Dachez and Alain Bauer

Perhaps one should speak not of Freemasonry but of Freemasonries in the plural. In each country Masonic historiography has developed uniqueness, but it is safe to say that one of the highest levels of scholarship has been in France. This book is a case in point, as two of the best known French Masonic scholars present their own view of the worldwide evolution and challenging mysteries of the fraternity over the centuries.